Rabbit' 5

Written by Maribeth Boelts

Illustrated by Melissa Webb

Rabbit is feeling happy.
You can see her smile.

Rabbit is feeling sad.
You can see her cry.

Rabbit is feeling mad.
You can see her frown.

Rabbit is feeling silly.
You can see her laugh.

Rabbit is feeling tired.
You can see her yawn.

Rabbit is sleeping.

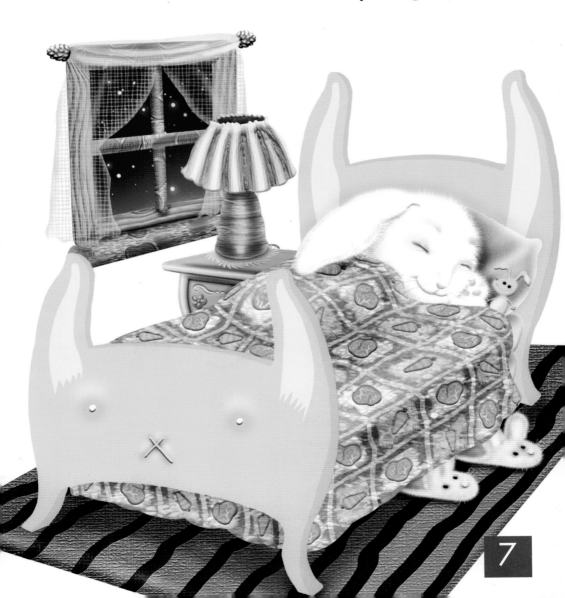

You can hear her snore!